BULLS LEGENDS ALPHABET

Words by Robin Feiner

A is for **A**rtis Gilmore.
A powerhouse in the paint,
this legend measured taller
than 7 feet. A gentle giant off
the court, The A-Train was a
four-time All-Star during his
1976–82 Chicago career.
Gilmore's super strength,
shooting touch, and fearless
rebounding landed him in
the Hall of Fame.

B is for **B**enny the Bull. This high-flying legend's family has entertained fans for more than 50 years. His Great Grandpa Benny was the NBA's first mascot back in 1969. Since 2004, today's Benny has wowed fans with acrobatic dunks, silly pranks, and sweet dance moves.

C is for **C**het 'The Jet' Walker. This legendarily speedy scorer was unstoppable in the open court. Walker starred on both ends for the Bulls, playing tough defense and averaging over 20 points per game. A four-time All-Star with Chicago, he only missed 18 games in six Bulls seasons.

D is for Luol Deng.
A beloved Bull of the 2000s
and 2010s, Deng was a
relentless worker who helped
Chicago make the playoffs in
eight of his 10 Bulls seasons.
But this two-time All-Star
is also known for his
legendary work with local
and international charities
and foundations, such as
Basketball Without Borders.

E is for **El**ton Brand.
The Bulls spiraled after
Michael Jordan's 1998
retirement. But Brand gave
fans something to cheer
about with his 1999–00
Rookie of the Year season.
The future looked bright –
until Chicago traded him
after his second season in
a move that left fans angry
and confused.

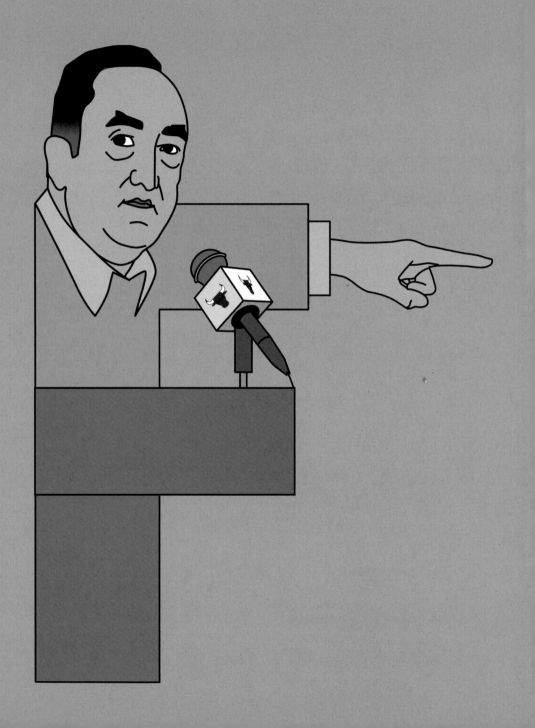

F is for Gar **F**orman.
Half of the infamous GarPax
leadership duo along with
John Paxson, Chicago made
the playoffs in seven of his
10 years as general manager.
But his legendarily bad draft,
trade, and signing decisions
caused many fans to see
him as the reason why star
players wouldn't come to
the Bulls.

G is for Horace **G**rant. Sporting his legendary goggles, this hard-nosed shot-blocker and rebounder provided skilled size, toughness, and defense during the Bulls' first three-peat of titles from 1990–93. His block on Kevin Johnson to seal the Bulls' third championship remains iconic decades later.

H is for Kirk **H**inrich. Captain Kirk wasn't a superstar. He arrived in 2003 with Chicago amidst one of the worst six-year stretches in NBA history. But his legendary work ethic and leadership were crucial for the Baby Bulls' eventual success. He retired with the most threes and third-most assists in team history.

I is for **I**vica Dukan.
This international scout isn't a household name. But for over 30 years he's scoured Europe for talent. It was The Duke who made the legendary move to bring over Croatian Toni Kukoč, a key piece of the second three-peat and 1995–96 Sixth Man of the Year.

J is for Jerry Sloan. The incredible Mr. Bull wasn't the most athletic, but always one of the hardest working. Sloan personified the city's down-to-earth toughness. This fearless legend's 10-year Chicago career started with the first Bulls team in 1966. His 4 was the team's first number ever retired.

K is for Stacey **K**ing. King played on three straight Bulls title teams from 1990–93. But his beloved broadcasting career that started in 2006 made him a true legend. King's enthusiasm and an endless string of 'Kingism' catchphrases and nicknames bring an extra level of fun to Chicago hoops.

**L is for Luc Longley.
This towering center was
a bit of a fish out of water
when he joined the Bulls in
1993. But after some hard
lessons from Michael Jordan,
Longley provided some
legendary defense down
low during the Bulls' second
three-peat from 1995–98
that had fans chanting
"Luuuuuuuuc."**

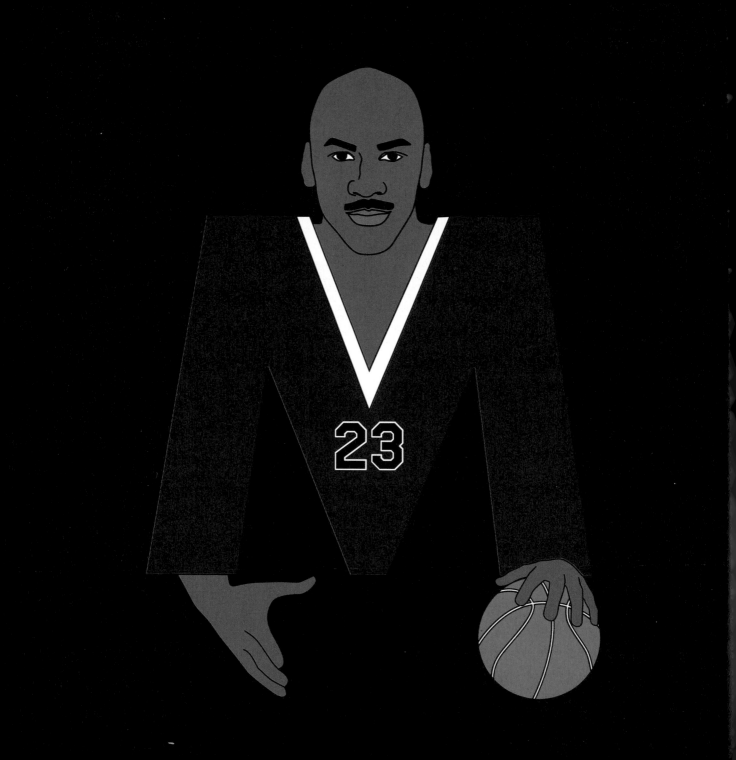

M is for Michael Jordan. His Airness is widely considered the greatest hooper ever. From The Flu Game, The Shrug, and The Shot, to his dunks, defense, and determination, M.J. supplied numerous legendary moments. His two three-peats, five MVPs, and 10 scoring titles make him Chicago – and NBA – royalty.

N is for Joakim **Noah.**
Jo was the heart and soul
of Tom Thibodeau's gritty,
title-contending Bulls squads
of the 2010s. The outspoken
center was the backbone
of the team's legendary
defense. Noah's shot was
ugly. But his pretty passing
helped teammates Luol Deng
and Derrick Rose shine.

O is for Charles Oakley. This rebounding machine was a legendary enforcer, sticking up for Michael Jordan in his early years. Oak was always ready to get to work, averaging a double-double in his four Chicago seasons – and getting into plenty of scraps along the way.

P is for Phil Jackson.
One of the sport's all-time greatest coaches, The Zen Master's legendary ability to stay calm and connect with players helped convince superstar Michael Jordan the Triangle Offense was best for the team. Chicago then won six titles in Jackson's nine seasons in charge from 1989–98.

Q is for Mr. Fourth **Q**uarter. Ben Gordon often saved his best for last. From his 2006 home buzzer-beater to down the Knicks, to his 2009 playoff heroics against the Celtics, and plenty in between, BG came through in the clutch time and again in his five Chicago seasons.

R is for Derrick **R**ose. Unbelievable athleticism, incredible ability to blow by defenders, and phenomenal finishing cemented Rose as a Bulls icon. The 2011 MVP was the engine of successful Bulls teams of the early 2010s. But Rose's 2012 playoffs injury remains a legendary what if?

S is for **S**cottie Pippen. While their offensive and defensive combination dominated, Pip was way more than Michael Jordan's sidekick. In 11 seasons from 1987–98, Pippen was a 10-time All-Defense and seven-time All-Star. Though sometimes still underappreciated, it's obvious: there are no three-peats without Scottie.

T is for Tom Thibodeau. Stalking the sideline and barking assignments, Thibs worked just as hard as his players. This legend's defense-first coaching style brought winning back to Chicago that fans hadn't seen in years. The 2011 Coach of the Year, the old-school Thibodeau pushed his players' minutes to the limit.

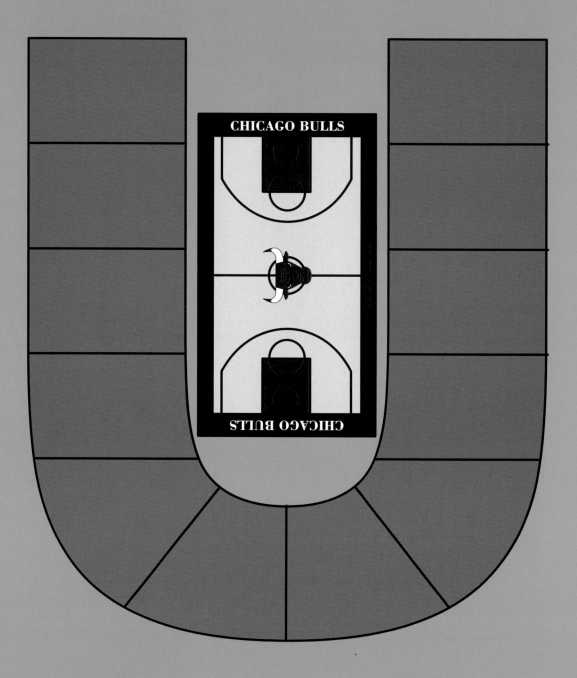

Uu

U is for the **U**nited Center. The House That Jordan Built, the United Center is where the Bulls have played their home games since 1994. It replaced Chicago Stadium. The Bulls' clinching of their fourth and fifth titles are just two of the legendary moments to take place here.

V is for Norm **V**an Lier. An All-Star in three of seven Chicago seasons, Stormin' Norman was one tough competitor. He was All-Defense each Bulls season, forming a fan-favorite tenacious tandem alongside Jerry Sloan in the 1970s. Van Lier also has the fourth most assists in Bulls franchise history.

W is for The **W**orm.
While Michael and Scottie flashed their skills, Dennis Rodman did the dirty work. The Worm's legendary rebounding and defending were matched by his giant personality, with his off-court antics and revolving hair color earning as much attention as his Hall-of-Fame play.

X is for John Paxson.
He was responsible for some legendary Bulls moments before becoming part of the resented GarPax leadership duo. From perfect shooting to help clinch the 1991 title to his series-sealing three in Game 5 of the 1993 Finals, Pax the player lives on in Chicago hoops history.

Y is for Thaddeus **Y**oung. During his two-year stop with the Bulls from 2019–21, Young was a model veteran who helped younger players grow. He led by example, earning the 2020–21 Hustle Award with his dedication to the little things – such as drawing charges and recovering loose balls.

Zz

Z is for **Z**ach LaVine.
A massive dunker, LaVine
reached new heights after
joining Chicago in 2017. In
2020–21, he set career highs
in points, rebounds, and
assists en route to his first
All-Star Game. And the next
season he helped the team
return to the playoffs after
a four-year drought.

The ever-expanding legendary library

EXPLORE THESE LEGENDARY ALPHABETS & MORE AT WWW.ALPHABETLEGENDS.COM

BULLS LEGENDS ALPHABET
www.alphabetlegends.com

Published by Alphabet Legends Pty Ltd in 2023
Created by Beck Feiner
Copyright © Alphabet Legends Pty Ltd 2023

Printed and bound in China.

9780645851410

ALPHABET LEGENDS